D0200986

TWISTED WHISKERS™ CHEER UP!

Twisted Whiskers™
Cheer Up!

RUNNING PRESS
PHILADELPHIA • LONDON

Library of Congress Control Number: 20055930822

ISBN 978-0-7624-2512-9

This book may be ordered by mail from the publisher.
Please include $1.00 for postage and handling.
But try your bookstore first!

Running Press Book Publishers
2300 Chestnut Street
Philadelphia, PA 19103-4371

Visit us on the web!
www.runningpress.com

INTRODUCTION

Where does your happiness lie? Chances are if you're reading this book it's been a little misplaced lately. There are many obstacles we encounter in our everyday lives in our constant quest for happiness and well-being, no matter how elusive it may seem. The most important thing to remember is, you are not alone! Sometimes when feeling down about work, school, friends, family, relationships—or simply bad hair!—all it takes is a little bit of goofiness and a smile to get your day back on the right track.

Take it from the **TWISTED WHISKERS**™ gang—they too have bad days riddled with frustration and mishaps, but somehow they manage to keep their heads—and their tails—up. Inside you'll find simple wisdom combined with the irresistible, quirky photographs of some of the most twisted furry friends you've ever laid eyes on. Often strange but always inspirational, **TWISTED WHISKERS**™ **CHEER UP!** is guaranteed to chase away even the most severe case of the blues.

Bad hair is the least
of my concerns.

Hang in there!

Having one of
those days?

Try changing
your perspective!

16

Stick it to 'em!

Stretching out
the good times.

Stay connected to
those who love you.

Dance your
cares away.

23

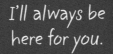

I'll always be
here for you.

Happiness is
touching your tongue
to your nose.

Add some color
to your world.

Don't forget to stop
and feel the breeze.

Feeling frazzled?

Things will
get better.

Hop to it!

Do you want to
talk about it?

Stop and listen to
your inner voice.

It can't be that
bad. . . right?

44

Tense?

It's a jungle
out there!

Happiness is
just a smile away.

Jump for joy!

Feline good!

Like a licking?

Don't let the twists
and turns of life
get you down.

Everybody feels a little
out of sorts sometimes.

Take time to stop and
smell everything!

Always have a positive attitude . . . and an excuse for everything.

Another good
hair day.
Woof, woof!

When it doubt, act happy—it will drive everyone nuts.

Take a break . . .
and achieve inner
harmony.

Everyone who
hates work . . .
raise your hand!

Lean on me.

Sooner or later,
it all ends up
at the bottom.

Sometimes you just need to let your hair down.

You've reached new heights . . . be proud of yourself!

I've seen you
overcome bigger
obstacles.

Did somebody say "weekend?!"

You're purrrfect.

I hate it when
that happens.

Always put your best
paw forward.

Getting my fur
and claws done
always makes me
feel fabulous.

Is it me or is everyone else crazy?

Have the courage
to be yourself.

Remember to paws
for reflection.

Going outside always makes me feel better.

Just relax . . .

Sometimes it's better to just smile and nod.

You scratch my back,
I'll scratch yours.

Turn that frown
upside down!

Chin up!

Try to focus on
what's important.

My head feels like it's going to explode!

Some days are just one big furball after another.

116

Let's go out
on the town.

I'm hoppin' that you
feel better soon.

Don't worry . . .
you'll spring back.

Biting off more than you can chew often leads to the greatest rewards.

Why the long face?

Life is short . . .
have fun!

This book has been bound
using handcraft methods and
Smyth-sewn to ensure durability.

The dust jacket and interior were
designed by Matt Goodman.

The text was edited
by Jennifer Leczkowski.

The text was set in
Spunky Jes and
Barnyard Gothic.